Dom
Columba
Marmion

Published by
Glenstal Publications,
Glenstal Abbey,
Co. Limerick

ISBN 1-872245-59-5

Contents

Abbot Columba Marmion

Joseph Marmion, the future Abbot Columba Marmion, was born in Dublin in 1885, the son of William Marmion and his wife, Herminie Cordier, a French woman.

When he was only fifteen he passed a scholarship examination entitling him to a place in Holy Cross College, Clonliffe, the Dublin Diocesan Seminary. His parents greatly encouraged his vocation.

He progressed well and was chosen for further studies in Rome where he was ordained in 1881. While in Rome he visited Monte Cassino which started him thinking of becoming a Benedictine monk. However, through ill health he returned to Ireland and was appointed curate in Dundrum, where he stayed for one year before taking up a professorship at Clonliffe College, and remained there four years until he entered the Benedictine Abbey of Maredsous in Belgium in 1886.

Some parishioners in Dundrum showed their appreciation of the parish's association with Marmion when in 1969 they founded the Dom Marmion Society which looks after the senior citizens of the area, and brings them to their purpose-built Dom Marmion House for keep-fit exercises, bingo, refreshments and other entertainments.

The publication of these excerpts from his book '*Christ The Life Of The Soul*' is to commemorate his Beatification which takes place on September 3rd, 2000.

The Kingdom

The kingdom is being formed here on earth. It is only entered by Baptism. On earth we live in it by grace in faith, hope, and love; but the day will come when we shall contemplate its perfection in heaven. God has given us his Son so that his Son may become our brother, and that we may one day be his co-heirs and share in the riches of his grace and glory. God is ready to shed his graces as abundantly and as usefully as those he shed upon the first Christians. He does not love us less than he loved them. All the means of sanctification that they had we also have. Christ is our all; apart from him we have nothing. In him we have everything, for everything is summed up in him.

The Incarnate Word

God has shown himself even more wonderful in the restoration of his design than he had been in the creation. It is through Jesus, the Incarnate Word, that God will restore all things. He it is who will reconcile us with God and restore grace to us.

The divine design is to constitute Christ the head of all the redeemed in order that by him, with him, and in him, we may all arrive at union with God, and realise the supernatural holiness which God requires of us.

Grace

Grace is an interior quality produced in us by God giving divine life to the soul and making it pleasing to God. Just as, in the natural domain, genius and science are qualities of the mind, beauty and strength are qualities of the body, loyalty and courage are qualities of the heart. Participation in this divine life is brought about by grace making us capable of knowing God as God knows himself, and of loving God as God loves himself.

O Heavenly Father, grant that I may preserve within my soul the grace that makes me your child.

The Trinity

Our holiness is to consist in adhering to God known and loved not only simply as author of creation, but as he knows and loves himself in the Trinity. This is to be united to God to the point of sharing his intimate life.

Consider the greatness of the gift he makes us. Look at the natural order. Minerals do not live; their mode of being is very inferior. Plants grow and live in accordance with fixed laws. The life of an animal is limited to instinct. Man is raised to a higher sphere; reason and free will characterise the life of a human being, but man is also matter. Above him is the angel, a pure spirit whose life reaches the highest degree in the scale of creation.

United To Christ

The soul that does not possess grace is not united to Christ; it does not draw from him the sap of sanctifying grace which would make it supernaturally fruitful. Christ alone is the source of our spiritual life; all our activity, all our existence has no value for eternal life unless we are united to Christ by grace.

Grace is the sap that rises from the root to the branches. It is not the root or the trunk that bears fruit; it is the branch, but the branch united by the trunk to the root, and drawing from the root the sap that nourishes. Break off the branch, separate it from the trunk, and no longer receiving the sap, it withers and becomes dead wood, incapable of producing fruit.

Need Of Faith

Jesus Christ had no need of faith. This virtue only exists in a soul not yet enjoying the vision of God. Since the soul of Christ contemplated God face to face it could not exercise faith in regard to this God whom it saw.

Neither had Jesus, properly speaking, the virtue of hope. It is no longer possible to hope for what is already possessed. The virtue of hope makes us desire the possession of God while giving us the confidence of receiving the graces necessary to arrive at this possession.

Perfection

Christ is not only the model of all perfection, he is also the cause of our sanctification. Christ is for us the source of grace, because having paid all our debt to divine justice by his life, passion and death, he has merited to distribute all grace to us. He practised charity to a supreme degree. The heart of Christ is an immense furnace of love. All his life can be summed up in these words: 'I do always the things that please my Father.'

Suffering

Christ shows his willingness to suffer throughout his life. The hour of his sacrifice is always present to him; he awaits it with impatience. He calls it 'his hour' as if it were the only one that counted for him in his earthly existence. He announces his death to his disciples; he traces out its details to them in advance, in such clear terms that they cannot be deceived. When Peter, deeply moved at the thought of seeing his master die, wishes to save him, Jesus rebukes him saying: 'Your thoughts don't come from God but from man.'

Faint-Hearted Souls

Why is it that faint-hearted souls are to be found who say that holiness is not for them, that perfection is something beyond their power; who say, when one speaks to them of perfection, 'It is not for me, I could never arrive at sanctity'? Do you know what makes them say that? It is their lack of faith in the effectiveness of Christ's merits. For it is the will of God that all should be holy. By ourselves we can do nothing without Christ, whether it concerns great things or small. But by dying for us, Christ has given us free and confident access to the Father, and through him there is no grace for which we cannot hope.

Weaknesses

Of ourselves we are weak. In the world of souls there are weaknesses of all kinds, but that is not a reason to be discouraged. These weaknesses, when they are not wilful, rather entitle us to Christ's mercy. See the unfortunate who wish to receive the pity of those from whom they ask alms. Far from hiding their poverty, they make a display of their rags and show their sores. That is what entitles them to the charity and compassion of the passer-by. For us, also, as for the sick who were brought to Christ when he lived in Judea, it is weakness confessed in his sight that draws down his mercy. When we humbly acknowledge our weakness and lean on his strength, the Father looks on us with love and with joy, because by this we proclaim that his Son, Jesus, is the one mediator whom he has willed to give to the world.

Spiritual Life

The more we read scripture, the more we see one great design stand out and dominate all things: this is that Christ Jesus, true God and true Man, is the centre of creation and redemption, and that everything relates to him, that through him every grace is given to us and all glory given to his father.

The contemplation of our Lord is not only holy but it makes us holy, Even only to think of him, to look at him with faith and love, sanctifies us. Christ is not one of the means of spiritual life; he is all our spiritual life.

The Divine Life

Those who keep their eyes fixed on Christ see, in his light, all that in them is opposed to the expansion of the divine life. They then seek in Jesus the strength to put away these obstacles so as to please him. They ask him to be the support of their weakness, to give and ever to increase in them the desire of always seeking to do that which is pleasing to his Father. They have neither the temptation to be discouraged when they fall through frailty, because they know too well that of themselves they can do nothing, nor the temptation to take the least pride in their progress, because they know that it is to Christ who dwells, lives and acts in them that they owe their perfection.

Master Of His Gifts

Christ, being God, is master of his gifts and of the manner in which he distributes them. We are no more able to limit his power than we are to determine how he will act. Christ can, when it seems good to him, cause grace to flow directly into the soul. The lives of the saints are full of these examples. The normal way in which Christ's grace comes to us is through the sacraments.

The Masterpiece

Look at an artist in his studio. With his chisel he hews and sculptures the marble in order to realise the ideal that haunts his genius.

When the masterpiece is finished, one could say that the artist created it but the chisel was the instrument that transmitted the artist's idea. The work is due to the chisel, but it was guided by the master's hand, itself directed by the genius which conceived the work.

So it is with the sacraments, they are the signs that produce grace, not as the principal cause, it is from Christ alone that sanctifying grace flows.

Fountains Of Salvation

Let us come with joy to draw at these fountains of salvation. Draw from these wholesome waters, enlarge the capacity of your souls by repentance, humility, confidence and, above all, by love, so that the action of the sacrament becomes deeper, vaster, and more lasting. Each time we approach the sacraments, let us renew our faith in the riches of Christ.

Aim Of All Our Life

We shall only grasp the mystery of Christ's action if we fix our attention upon the Spirit and his action within us. The aim of all our life is to enter with great humility into God's thoughts and to adapt ourselves to them as perfectly as possible with childlike simplicity. To enter into God's plan, we must not only receive Christ but, as St Paul points out, we must also 'receive the Holy Spirit' and yield to his action so as to be 'one with Christ.'

God's Will

It is not always enough for us to know God's will. Due to our fallen nature, we often need strength to carry into effect what God requires of us. It is the Holy Spirit who, by the gift of fortitude, sustains us in particularly difficult moments. There are timid souls that fear the trials of the inner life. They are so much the deeper in proportion as God calls us higher, but let us fear nothing.

Holiness

Holiness for us is nothing else than the complete unfolding, the full development of the grace given to us at baptism. The substance of all holiness is to draw from this initial grace all the blessings which it contains and that God causes to flow from it. From the moment of this infusion of grace in us by baptism the Holy Spirit abides in us with the Father and the Son. Grace makes our soul the temple of the Holy Trinity.

The inspirations of the Holy Spirit have no other end than to mould us to a greater resemblance to Jesus. We should not doubt his goodness and love, or be heedless to the benefits of his grace.

Faith

Faith is the virtue that Jesus claims from those who approach him. It is the basis of all our spiritual life. As long as we are on earth God should be for us a hidden God to be known, adored and served by faith. The greater our faith is, the more we are pleasing to God.

When we let ourselves be guided by the Holy Spirit, and are faithful to his inspirations, even in our weakness the action of the Spirit can produce much fruit. If Jesus Christ has merited all for us, it is by his Spirit that he guides and directs us.

Supreme Truth

Faith is our intelligence affirming the word of God to be the supreme truth. The divine word affirms the existence of mysteries beyond our reason. Faith can be required from us in things where our senses, our experience, seem to tell us the very contrary of what God tells us, but God requires our conviction in the authority of his revelation to be so absolute that if all creation affirmed the contrary we should say to God, in spite of everything, 'My God, I believe because you say it.'

Baptism

We receive the gift of faith in baptism, but we must not leave it buried deep in our heart. We must ask God to increase it in us. Faith penetrates through the veil of the humanity that hides the divinity of Christ from our sight. Whether he be shown to us in a crib, under the form of a little child, or in a workshop, or under the species of bread and wine, faith tells us that it is always the same Christ, true God and true Man.

When you enter a church and see the little lamp burning before the tabernacle announcing the presence of Jesus Christ, do not let your genuflection be a mere ceremony performed out of routine, but a homage of intimate faith as if you saw him in all the splendour of his eternal glory.

Faith Is A Seed

Faith is a seed, and every seed contains in germ the future harvest. Provided that we put away from faith all that can diminish and tarnish it, and develop it by prayer and practice manifested in love, we have the substance of the joys to come.

Behind In The Tomb

As Christ left the winding sheet behind him in the tomb, so have we left all our sins in the baptismal waters. In the same way that Christ came forth free and living from the sepulchre, so we have come forth from the sacred font, not only purified from all sin, but with a soul adorned with grace. This God-given life is only in a state of germ. It must grow and develop in the same way as our renunciation of sin is renewed and sustained.

Grace

St Paul, in his letter to his disciple Timothy, encourages him to stir up the grace of God he received at his ordination. We should also stir up in ourselves the grace received at baptism, by renewing the promises then made. For example, when, after communion while Jesus is really present in our hearts, we repent of our sins and attach ourselves only to Christ, then the grace of baptism springs up from the depths of our souls, where the sign of baptism remains indelibly engraved.

Gratitude

Gratitude is the first feeling that baptismal grace should cause to arise within us. Joy is the second. We should have a deep sense of gladness when we think of our baptism, the day God looked upon us with love and called us to share in the blessings that overflow from Christ.

Our Thoughts

To speak the truth is to express something that is in accordance with our thoughts. An object is true when there is harmony between what it ought to be and what it is in reality. Gold is true when it possesses all the properties that we know to belong to the nature of this metal. It is false when it has the appearance but not the properties of gold. To be true, which is the first condition necessary in order to be pleasing to God, each human action must conform to our condition as free and reasonable creatures, subject to God. Otherwise the action does not correspond to our nature.

The Universe

Consider the universe around you. God finds his glory in all creatures, but only when they are conformed to the laws that rule their nature. The stars of heaven praise God in silence by their orderly movement in space; the waters of the sea praise him by not overpassing the limits he has assigned to them; the earth by keeping the laws of its stability; the trees by producing blossoms and fruits after their kind; the animals by fulfilling the instincts placed in them by their creator.

Like all creatures, man was made to glorify God, but he can only glorify him by acts that agree with his nature. It is in exercising our own faculties - intelligence, will, love, feelings and imagination - that our human nature performs its actions, and these actions are raised by grace to the point of being worthy of God.

Our Nature As Free

We must remain ourselves and live in a manner which conforms to our nature as free and reasonable creatures. We must keep our individual personality in our supernatural life, all that is good in it, that is a part of the 'truth' - that sincerity which the life of grace demands.

Holiness is not a single mould where one's natural qualities have to disappear so that only a uniform type may be represented. God, in creating us, endowed each of us with gifts, talents and privileges. Each soul has its special natural beauty: one shines by depth of intelligence, another is distinguished by strength of will. Grace respects this beauty, as it respects the nature on which it is based. It will just add a supernatural splendour to the natural beauty, transfiguring it.

Our Vocation

In order to be 'in the truth' we must be true to our vocation. Grace cannot be in contradiction to this. It would be untrue to her state for a mother of a family to pass long hours in church when her presence is required at home in caring for her family. It would be untrue to his vocation for a religious to spend an hour in private devotions instead of the work prescribed at that hour. 'Sanctify them in truth' was the prayer of Jesus at the Last Supper for his disciples.

Manhood

A child is not born to remain always a child. The law of his nature is that he should come to the age of manhood. The supernatural life is no exception to this law. Jesus could bring us to the degree of holiness that he has destined for our souls by taking control of our wills. Although Jesus' merits are the cause of all sanctification and his grace is the principle of all supernatural life, we have free will to do our part in the work of our perfection, or not.

It is true that supernatural love is not grace, but love and grace always go together. Grace elevates our being and love transforms our activity. The degree of one marks the degree of the other, and every grave fault, of whatever nature it may be, kills grace and love in us.

Obscurity

Until the age of thirty Jesus lived a life of labour and obscurity in the workshop at Nazareth. During these years he did nothing extraordinary to attract the eyes of the world. He lived in very simple labour, and yet this labour was infinitely pleasing to his Father, because everything was done for his glory.

Act Out Of Love

Look around you. You can meet two pious people in the state of grace who lead side by side the same kind of life. Both perform outwardly the same material actions, and yet there may be an enormous difference between them in the eyes of God.

One person, attentive to God, acts with great love. She acts only to please God. The other does the same work but in this person faith is asleep. She does not think of God's interest. The measure of this merit is small. It is diminished by self love and vanity.

Precious Gift

The gift of understanding makes us search deeply into the truths of faith. Every baptised soul possesses within itself this precious gift. You read a text of scripture. You have read and reread it many times without having been struck by it but, one day, a sudden light flashes, illuminating to its depths the truth set forth in the text. This truth then becomes altogether clear to you and often a principle of supernatural life and action. It is an intuition of the Holy Spirit who, by the gift of understanding, makes you penetrate further into the deep meaning of the revealed truths so that you may hold them more firmly.

Pure Intention

Purity of intention keeps our soul in the presence of God and urges us to seek him alone in all things. It prevents curiosity, levity, vanity, self-love, pride and ambition from entering into our actions so as to diminish their merit.

A pure intention, frequently renewed, surrenders the soul to God in its being and in its activity, and so, by each good work it causes to be done and referred to God, it increases the life of the soul.

Human Activity

Jesus Christ exercised every form of human activity. We must not think of Our Lord as living rapt in ecstasy. On the contrary, he found the driving power of his activity in the beatific vision of his Father. He willed to glorify his Father by sanctifying in his person the forms of activity we ourselves have to exert.

We pray; he passed the nights in prayer.

We work; he toiled in labour till the age of thirty.

We eat; he sat at table with his disciples.

We suffer; he has shed tears.

We experience joy; his holy soul felt great joy.

We take rest; sleep has likewise closed his eyelids.

In a word, he has done all we do. Jesus has done all this to merit for us the power of sanctifying all our acts.

Temptation

Our Lord demands that the brightness of our works be such that it leads those who behold it to glorify his Father.

Do not let us fear temptation. God makes it profitable for us when we resist it, because it is the occasion of a victory that strengthens us in the love of God. Neither let us fear trials. We may pass through great difficulties, undergo serious contradictions and endure deep sufferings, but from the moment we begin to serve God through love these difficulties and sufferings serve to nourish love.

As long as we are here on earth we can always grow in grace. The river of divine life began to flow in us on the day of baptism, but it can ever go on increasing for the joy of our soul, which it waters and fertilises, until this river flows into the divine ocean.

Contact With God

The essential element of prayer is the supernatural contact of the soul with God, from whom it absorbs that divine life that is the source of all holiness. This contact is produced when the soul, raised by faith and love, supported by Jesus Christ, yields itself to God, to his will, through the movement of the Holy Spirit. No reasoning, no purely natural effort, can produce this contact. This contact is produced in the darkness of faith, but it fills the soul with light and life. Saint Benedict makes it clearly understood that a life of prayer is absolutely necessary in order to find God.

Heart Prayer

Prayer only really begins at the moment when the will, set on fire with love, enters supernaturally into contact with the divine Good, yielding itself lovingly to God in order to please him and fulfil his precepts and desire. It is in the heart that prayer essentially dwells.

Some people reap more fruit from a simple reading, interspersed with aspirations of the heart, than from an exercise where the reason enters almost exclusively into play.

Vocal Prayer

There are some far advanced in spiritual ways who can never enter into prayer without the help of a book. Reading serves to put them in the right atmosphere for prayer; it would be a mistake for them to do without it. There are others who can only commune with God through vocal prayer; they would be ill at ease if led into another way. However, as a general rule, it remains true that in the same measure as one progresses in the light of faith and in fidelity, the action of the Holy Spirit increases within the soul and there is ever less need of having recourse to reasoning in order to find God.

Spiritual Ways

The moments in the day that the soul consecrates exclusively to the formal exercise of prayer are only the intensifying of a state in which it remains habitually, but gently, united to God, speaking to him interiorly and listening to the voice from on high. This state is more than the simple presence of God. It is an intimate intercourse, full of love, in which the soul speaks to God, sometimes with the lips, most often from the heart, and remains intimately united to him, despite the variety of the day's work and occupations.

There are many souls, simple and upright, who, faithful to the attraction of the Holy Spirit, arrive at this desirable state.

'Lord teach us to pray.'

Contemplation

Desire with all your strength to possess a high degree of prayer and to enjoy perfect contemplation. However, we ought to subject this desire to the will of God. He alone knows what is best for our souls, and while not sparing our efforts to remain generously and humbly faithful to present grace, it is extremely important to keep always in peace, assured as we are of God's goodness and wisdom in regard to each one of us. Contemplation leads us to the most pure, simple and perfect knowledge of God.

Distractions

A light, scattered soul, one habitually distracted and making no effort to repress the wanderings of the imagination, will never be a soul of prayer. During prayer itself we should not disturb ourselves about the distractions that may arrive, but remain faithful and lead the mind gently back to the subject that should be occupying us. Outward solitude and interior detachment are necessary for prayer, because it is the Holy Spirit who prays in us, and his action in the soul is extremely delicate.

The Sentence

From the mouth of Jesus himself we know that the sentence which will decide our eternal lot will be founded on the love we have had for Jesus Christ in the person of our brethren. When we appear before Christ on the last day, he will not ask us if we have fasted a great deal, if we have passed our life in penance, if we have given many hours to prayer; no, but if we have loved and helped our brethren.

The Incarnation

There are souls that seek God in Jesus Christ, and accept the humanity of Christ, but stop there. That is not sufficient.

We must accept the Incarnation with all the consequences it involves; we must not let the gift of ourselves stop at Christ's own humanity but extend it to his mystical body. Never forget this, for it is one of the most important points of the supernatural life: to abandon the least of our brethren is to abandon Christ himself.

All Are Called

Charity excludes no one, for Christ died for all, and all are called to belong to his kingdom. Charity embraces even sinners, because the possibility remains of them again becoming living members of Christ's body.

Love has to take different forms according to our neighbour's state; our love, in fact, should not be a platonic love, of theory alone, but a love that translates itself into appropriate acts.

The Psalms

Read the Psalms. You will see how these canticles, inspired by the Holy Spirit, relate, proclaim and exalt all the perfections of God. The canticle of the eternal Word in the Holy Trinity is simple yet infinite but, upon the lips of creatures incapable of comprehending the infinite, praises are multiplied and repeated.

With wonderful and great variety of expression, the Psalms sing by turn of the power, magnificence, holiness, goodness, mercy and beauty of God.

The Eucharist

If Jesus instituted the eucharist in order to unite himself to us and make us live by his life, we can be sure that the sacrament contains all that is needful to bring about this union.

In this marvellous invention the incomparable effect to produce in us a divine transformation is hidden.

Source of Text

The excerpts are taken from
'*Christ The Life Of The Soul*'
by Dom Columba Marmion.

'*Christ The Life Of The Soul*' is a
collection of conferences that comprise
instructions and meditations given during
retreats to his community, which were
translated from the original French text
into English by a nun of Tyburn convent.

Sources of the excerpts taken from
Part 1, *The Divine Economy*, and from
Part II, *Foundation and Double Aspect
of The Christian Life,* are listed on pages
55 and 56.

Excerpt Title	Chapter	Conference Title
The Kingdom	1.1	The Divine Plan of Our Adoptive Predestination
The Incarnate Word	1.1	in Jesus Christ.
Grace	1.1	
The Trinity	1.1	
United To Christ	1.1	
Need Of Faith	1.2	
Perfection	1.3	Christ, the Only Model of All Perfection. Christ the Author of
Suffering	1.3	Our Redemption.
Faint Hearted	1.3	
Weaknesses	1.4	
Spiritual Life	1.4	Christ the Efficient Cause of All grace
Divine Life	1.4	
Master Of His Gifts	1.4	
The Masterpiece	1.4	
Fountains of Salvation	1.4	
Aim Of All Our Life	1.6	
God's Will	1.6	The Holy Spirit. the Spirit of Jesus.
Holiness	1.6	
Faith	2.1	Faith in Jesus Christ the Foundation of Christian Life.